EASY FOIL Recipes

EASY FOIL Recipes

Publications International, Ltd.

Favorite Brand Name Recipes at www.fbnr.com

Photography on pages 15, 19, 27, 31, 41, 45, 49, 65, 81, 83, 85 and 87 by Peter Dean Ross Photographs.

Recipe development on pages 14, 16, 26, 33, 48, 64 and 70 by Susan Garard.
Recipe development on pages 18, 32, 38 and 40 by Gregg Hollander.
Recipe development on pages 30, 44, 47, 80, 88 and 90 by Nancy Ross Ryan.
Recipe development on pages 39, 84, 86 and 89 by Karen Straus.

Pictured on the front cover *(clockwise from top left):* Sweet & Sour Chicken *(page 64),* Baked Cinnamon Apple *(page 80),* Spicy Pistachio Chicken *(page 10)* and Chicken with Cornbread Dumplings *(page 40).*

Pictured on the back cover: Apricot Pork Chop and Dressing *(page 44).*

ISBN: 1-4127-2127-X

Manufactured in China.

8 7 6 5 4 3 2 1

Microwave Cooking: Microwave ovens vary in wattage. Use the cooking times as guidelines and check for doneness before adding more time.

Preparation/Cooking Times: Preparation times are based on the approximate amount of time required to assemble the recipe before cooking, baking, chilling or serving. These times include preparation steps such as measuring, chopping and mixing. The fact that some preparations and cooking can be done simultaneously is taken into account. Preparation of optional ingredients and serving suggestions is not included.

Contents

Foil Cooking

Simply Delicious Foil Recipes

It's one of those days—everyone's on a different dinner schedule and you're wondering how you can avoid serving reheated, dried-out meals to the latecomers. Let foil packets come to the rescue! With packet cooking you can prepare individual servings, wrap them in foil and hold them in the refrigerator until you're ready to cook—no more reheating food for dinner stragglers. You can create delicious dinners easily and quickly and keep cleanup to a minimum when you cook in foil.

Easy Foil Recipes includes dozens of recipes for cooking or grilling in foil packets. In addition, discover the convenience of cooking in foil bags, lining baking pans with foil, and baking in foil cups. You'll be surprised how quick and easy foil cooking can be.

Foil Packet Cooking

What is foil packet cooking? Wrap ingredients in foil to create packets, then cook them in a hot oven or on the grill. Packets can serve one or more. Recipes for one or two can be prepared in most toaster ovens, which will help to keep the kitchen cool and save energy. Vegetable packets can be tossed on the grill while the steaks or burgers are grilling. You'll love the convenience of this cooking method. Packets can be prepared ahead of time and cooked when needed. There are no pots and pans to scrub and the oven stays clean, too. You can even customize individual packets for fussy eaters—simply prepare one packet without the mushrooms that one family member dislikes.

Packet Basics

◆ Measure and tear off a foil sheet(s) as directed in the recipe and place it on the countertop.

◆ Spray the foil with nonstick cooking spray or grease with butter or margarine as directed in the recipe. In most cases a light spraying is sufficient, but sticky or sugary foods may require a generous coating.

◆ Preheat the oven, toaster oven or the grill.

◆ Place the ingredients in the center of the foil sheets as the recipe directs.

◆ Wrap foil around the ingredients, leaving room for heat to circulate. Bring the two sides together above the food; double fold the foil and crimp to seal as shown in the top photograph.

◆ Double fold the remaining ends and crimp to seal the packet (bottom photograph).

◆ Place the foil packets on a baking sheet, toaster oven tray or a baking pan with 1-inch-high sides.

◆ Bake the packets on the baking sheet on center rack as directed. Or, slide the packets onto the grill.

◆ Remove packets from the oven. The foil packets will be very hot so use oven mitts when handling them. Carefully open one end of each packet to avoid the escaping steam. Allow some of the steam to escape before completely opening the packet. Check the food for doneness; rewrap and return to the oven if the food isn't completely cooked.

◆ Transfer the contents of the packets to serving plates or a serving dish. When cooking single-serve packets of food, you may eat right out of the packet if you wish.

Double fold foil and crimp tightly to seal.

Double fold each end of packet and crimp tightly to seal.

Large Foil Bags

Foil bags large enough to hold a turkey are available at most supermarkets. Use these bags for large items such as turkeys, roasting chickens, beef roasts and pork roasts. Add vegetables to the bag and you have almost an entire meal prepared quickly and conveniently. Cleanup is easy, too.

Other Uses of Foil in the Kitchen

Lining baking pans with foil: When roasting meat or vegetables, first line the baking pan with foil to minimize cleanup. When baking bar cookies or brownies, line the baking pan with foil, allowing the edges of the foil sheet to overhang the edges of the pan. Grease the foil. After the bars or brownies are cool, simply lift them out of the pan using the foil.

Lining cookie sheets with foil: Place a sheet of foil on the cookie sheet when making cookies. Grease the foil if the recipe recommends greasing the cookie sheet. Place cookie dough on the foil and bake as directed. After removing cookies from the oven, slide the foil off the cookie sheet onto a wire rack or the countertop. Cool the cookie sheet and reuse it with another sheet of foil—the cookie sheet remains clean.

Covering with foil: Foil can be used to cover baking pans and casseroles during baking.

Cooking in a slow cooker: To easily lift a meatloaf or a casserole dish out of a slow cooker, make foil handles according to the following directions:

Cut three 18×3-inch strips of heavy-duty foil. Crisscross strips so they resemble the spokes of a wheel (top photograph). Place the dish or food in the center of the strips.

Pull foil strips up and over (bottom photograph) the food. Use the strips to lower the food into the slow cooker. Leave the strips in while you cook so you can easily lift them out again when finished cooking.

Crisscross the strips of foil like spokes of a wheel.

Pull foil strips up and over food.

Foil Bake Cups

Foil bake cups, like paper bake cups, are available in several sizes to line muffin pans when making muffins or cupcakes. The added bonus of foil bake cups is that they are rigid enough to be used without muffin pans. Simply place the bake cups on a baking sheet or in a baking pan with 1-inch sides.

Disposable Foil Baking Pans

Disposable foil baking pans are readily available in many sizes. Use them in place of a roasting pan for a holiday turkey or a Sunday-supper roast. Use them for transporting your favorite dish to the next pot-luck dinner or picnic. There's no need to worry about searching for your casserole dish when the meal's over. Bake bar cookies, brownies and sheet cakes in disposable foil pans if you plan to ship them to friends or family or take them to a bake sale.

From tasty main dishes, like Spicy Pistachio Chicken and Apricot Pork Chops and Dressing, to taste-tempting side dishes and quick-to-fix meal finales, like Cinnamon-Raisin-Banana Bread Pudding and Easy Gingerbread, you'll discover a variety of recipes that will simplify dinner preparation whether you're cooking for one or an on-the-go family. So roll out the foil and enjoy an easy-to-make, home-cooked meal tonight!

◆ Minutes to prepare, minutes to bake

◆ Make ahead, bake later

◆ Foil is versatile

◆ Cleanup is a snap!

Easy Entrées

Spicy Pistachio Chicken

4 TYSON® Individually Fresh Frozen® Boneless, Skinless Chicken Breasts
1 tablespoon unsalted butter, melted
¼ teaspoon cayenne pepper
¼ cup finely chopped pistachio nuts
1 tablespoon grated Parmesan cheese
1 tablespoon finely chopped green onion

PREP: Preheat oven to 350°F. Prepare 4 pieces of foil large enough for each to hold 1 chicken breast. CLEAN: Wash hands. Place each breast on piece of foil. Brush chicken with melted butter and sprinkle with pepper. Wrap foil around chicken. CLEAN: Wash hands.

COOK: Place foil packets on cookie sheet; bake 35 minutes. Remove from oven; open foil and sprinkle pistachio nuts over chicken. Leave foil open and return to oven. Bake about 5 minutes or until internal juices of chicken run clear. (Or insert instant-read meat thermometer in thickest part of chicken. Temperature should read 170°F.)

SERVE: Remove chicken from foil and place on serving platter. Sprinkle chicken with Parmesan cheese and green onion.

CHILL: Refrigerate leftovers immediately. *Makes 4 servings*

Prep Time: 10 minutes
Cook Time: 40 minutes

Steak San Marino

¼ cup all-purpose flour
1 teaspoon salt
½ teaspoon black pepper
1¼ pounds beef sirloin steak, about ¾ inch thick, cut into 4 pieces
1 can (8 ounces) tomato sauce
1 carrot, chopped
½ onion, chopped
1 rib celery, chopped
1 teaspoon dried Italian seasoning
½ teaspoon Worcestershire sauce
Hot cooked rice
4 sheets (18×12 inches) heavy-duty foil, lightly sprayed with nonstick
   cooking spray

1. Preheat oven to 450°F.

2. Combine flour, salt and pepper in small bowl. Coat beef in flour mixture. Place each piece of beef on foil. Combine tomato sauce, carrot, onion, celery, Italian seasoning and Worcestershire sauce in small bowl; pour a quarter of tomato sauce mixture over each piece of beef.

3. Double fold sides and ends of foil to seal packets, leaving head space for heat circulation. Place packets on baking sheet.

4. Bake 25 to 28 minutes or until beef is tender. Remove packets from oven. Carefully open one end of each packet to allow steam to escape. Open packets and transfer contents to serving plates. Serve steaks and sauce over rice. *Makes 4 servings*

Chicken Parmesan

2 boneless skinless chicken breasts
2 sheets (18×12 inches) heavy-duty foil, lightly sprayed with nonstick
    cooking spray
  Salt and black pepper
1 cup pasta sauce
½ cup chopped onion
8 slices zucchini, quartered
¼ cup (1 ounce) shredded mozzarella cheese
2 tablespoons grated Parmesan cheese
  Hot cooked spaghetti or linguine (optional)

1. Preheat toaster oven or oven to 450°F.

2. Place one chicken breast in center of each sheet of foil. Season to taste with salt and pepper.

3. Combine pasta sauce, onion and zucchini. Pour half of sauce mixture over each chicken breast. Sprinkle with cheeses. Double fold sides and ends of foil to seal packets, leaving head space for heat circulation. Place packets on toaster oven tray or baking sheet.

4. Bake 16 to 18 minutes until chicken is no longer pink in center. Remove from oven. Carefully open one end of each foil packet to allow steam to escape. Open packets and transfer contents to serving plates. Serve with spaghetti, if desired. *Makes 2 servings*

Turkey Loaf with Quick Foil Potatoes

1 pound ground turkey breast (99% fat-free)
1¼ cups finely chopped onion, divided
½ cup finely chopped celery
2 eggs, beaten
6 tablespoons chili sauce, divided
1 clove garlic, minced
½ teaspoon salt
Black pepper
4 cups frozen shredded hash brown potatoes
Black pepper
2 tablespoons butter, cut into pieces

1. Preheat oven to 375°F. Line 8×8-inch baking pan with foil; lightly spray with nonstick cooking spray. Set aside.

2. Combine turkey, ¾ cup onion, celery, eggs, 5 tablespoons chili sauce, garlic, salt and ⅛ teaspoon pepper in large bowl; mix well. Form turkey mixture into loaf in foil-lined baking pan. Spread remaining 1 tablespoon chili sauce on top of loaf.

3. Bake 50 to 55 minutes until juices run clear and thermometer inserted in center of loaf registers 170°F.

4. Meanwhile, lightly spray 1 sheet (18×12 inches) heavy-duty foil with cooking spray. Combine frozen hash browns, remaining ½ cup onion and pepper to taste in medium bowl; mix well.

5. Place hash brown mixture in center of foil. Dot with butter. Double fold sides and ends of foil to seal packet. Place packet on small baking sheet.

6. When turkey loaf has baked for 30 minutes, place foil packet in oven. Bake on baking sheet 25 minutes. Remove turkey loaf and foil packet from oven. Let stand 5 minutes. Carefully open one end of foil packet to allow steam to escape. Open packet and transfer mixture to serving plates. Serve with sliced turkey loaf.   *Makes 4 servings*

Single-Serve Dijon & Honey Pork Chop

½ teaspoon LAWRY'S® Seasoned Salt
1 pork chop, cut ½ inch thick
½ cup sliced carrot
½ cup sliced celery
¼ cup sliced mushrooms
3 tablespoons LAWRY'S® Dijon & Honey Marinade with Lemon Juice

Sprinkle Seasoned Salt on both sides of chop. In small bowl, combine remaining ingredients; mix well. Place chop on 12×9-inch piece heavy-duty aluminum foil. Top chop with vegetable mixture. Fold foil to enclose; seal tightly. Freeze. Remove packet from freezer when ready to cook. Place packet seam side up on baking sheet. Bake in 425°F oven 1 hour or until chop is no longer pink in center. To serve, carefully remove chop and vegetables—they will be very hot.   *Makes 1 serving*

Serving Suggestion: Place a potato in the oven at the same time as the pork chop packet—they'll be ready at the same time.

Vegetarian Orzo & Feta Bake

1 package (16 ounces) orzo pasta
1 can (4¼ ounces) chopped black olives, drained
2 cloves garlic, minced
1 sheet (24×18 inches) heavy-duty foil, lightly sprayed with nonstick cooking spray
1 can (about 14 ounces) diced Italian-style tomatoes
1 can (14 ounces) vegetable broth
2 tablespoons olive oil
6 to 8 ounces feta cheese, cut into ½-inch cubes

1. Preheat oven to 450°F.

2. Combine orzo, olives and garlic in medium bowl. Place orzo mixture in center of foil sheet.

3. Fold sides of foil up around orzo mixture, but do not seal.

4. In same bowl, combine tomatoes with juice, broth and oil. Pour over orzo mixture. Top with cheese.

5. Double fold sides and ends of foil to seal packet, leaving head space for heat circulation. Place packet on baking sheet.

6. Bake 22 to 24 minutes or until pasta is tender. Remove from oven. Let stand 5 minutes. Open packet and transfer contents to serving plates

Makes 6 servings (or 8 side dish servings)

Quick Tip

Using canned tomatoes that are already diced and canned olives that are already chopped is a great time saver when you are in a hurry to prepare dinner.

Red Snapper Scampi

¼ cup margarine or butter, softened
1 tablespoon white wine
1½ teaspoons minced garlic
½ teaspoon grated lemon peel
⅛ teaspoon black pepper
1½ pounds red snapper, orange roughy or grouper fillets
(about 4 to 5 ounces each)

1. Preheat oven to 450°F. Combine margarine, wine, garlic, lemon peel and pepper in small bowl; stir to blend.

2. Place fish on foil-lined shallow baking pan. Top with seasoned margarine. Bake 10 to 12 minutes or until fish begins to flake easily when tested with fork. *Makes 4 servings*

Tip: Serve fish over mixed salad greens, if desired. Or, add sliced carrots, zucchini and bell pepper cut into matchstick-size strips to the fish in the baking pan for an easy vegetable side dish.

Prep and Cook Time: 12 minutes

Garlicky Chicken Packets

1 cup julienned carrots
½ cup sliced onion
¼ cup chopped fresh basil *or* 1 tablespoon dried basil leaves
2 tablespoons mayonnaise
6 cloves garlic, minced
⅛ teaspoon black pepper
4 boneless skinless chicken breast halves

Cut foil into 4 (12-inch) squares. Fold squares in half.

Preheat oven to 400°F. Place a quarter of carrots and onion on 1 side of each foil square near fold. Combine basil, mayonnaise, garlic and pepper in small bowl; spread mixture on chicken. Place chicken, mayonnaise side up, on top of vegetables. Fold foil over chicken; seal by creasing and folding edges of foil. Place foil packets on baking sheet. Bake 20 to 25 minutes or until juices run clear and chicken is no longer pink in center. *Makes 4 servings*

That's Italian Meat Loaf

1 (8-ounce) can tomato sauce, divided
1 egg, lightly beaten
½ cup chopped onion
½ cup chopped green bell pepper
⅓ cup dry seasoned bread crumbs
2 tablespoons grated Parmesan cheese
½ teaspoon garlic powder
¼ teaspoon black pepper
1 pound ground beef
½ pound ground pork or veal
1 cup shredded Asiago cheese

Slow Cooker Directions

Reserve ⅓ cup tomato sauce; set aside in refrigerator. Combine remaining tomato sauce and egg in large bowl. Stir in onion, bell pepper, bread crumbs, Parmesan cheese, garlic powder and black pepper. Add ground beef and pork; mix well and shape into loaf.

Place meat loaf on foil strips (see page 8). Place in slow cooker. Cover and cook on LOW 8 to 10 hours or on HIGH 4 to 6 hours; internal temperature should read 170°F.

Spread meat loaf with reserved tomato sauce. Sprinkle with Asiago cheese. Cover and cook 15 minutes or until cheese is melted. Using foil strips, remove meat loaf from slow cooker. *Makes 8 servings*

Make-Ahead Dill Chicken in Foil

8 chicken thighs, skinned
1 teaspoon salt
½ teaspoon ground black pepper
½ cup butter or margarine, melted
2 tablespoons lemon juice
1 teaspoon dried dill weed
   Vegetable cooking spray
3 green onions, thinly sliced
1 cup thinly sliced carrots
6 ounces Swiss cheese, cut into 8 slices

Sprinkle chicken thighs with salt and pepper. Combine butter, lemon juice
and dill in small bowl. Cut four 12-inch squares of heavy-duty foil; coat
each with cooking spray. Place 1 tablespoon dill-butter sauce on center of
each foil square; place 2 chicken thighs on sauce. Divide onion and carrot
slices evenly over chicken. Top each with additional 1 tablespoon sauce
and 1 slice cheese. Fold foil into packets, sealing securely. Label, date
and freeze chicken until ready to bake.* To serve, place frozen foil packets
in baking pan and bake at 400°F 1 hour or until fork can be inserted into
chicken with ease and juices run clear, not pink.   *Makes 4 servings*

**Chicken may be frozen for up to 9 months. If serving immediately without freezing, place foil packets
in baking pan and bake at 400°F 35 to 40 minutes or until fork can be inserted into chicken with ease
and juices run clear, not pink.*

Favorite recipe from **National Chicken Council**

Quick Tip

Preparing single-serve foil meal packets and
freezing them for later use makes meal preparation
a breeze. When you don't feel like preparing a
meal for one or someone needs to eat early, just
pull a packet out of the freezer, pop it into the
oven and relax until dinner is ready.

Fiesta Beef Enchiladas

   6 ounces lean ground beef
¼ cup sliced green onions
   1 teaspoon fresh minced or bottled garlic
   1 cup (4 ounces) shredded reduced-fat Mexican cheese blend or Cheddar
      cheese, divided
¾ cup chopped tomato, divided
½ cup cold cooked white or brown rice
⅓ cup frozen corn, thawed
¼ cup salsa or picante sauce
   6 (6- to 7-inch) corn tortillas
   2 sheets (20×12 inches) heavy-duty foil, lightly sprayed with nonstick
      cooking spray
½ cup mild or hot red or green enchilada sauce
½ cup sliced romaine lettuce leaves

1. Preheat oven to 375°F. Cook ground beef in medium nonstick skillet over medium heat until no longer pink; drain. Add green onions and garlic; cook and stir 2 minutes.

2. Combine meat mixture, ¾ cup cheese, ½ cup tomato, rice, corn and salsa; mix well. Spoon mixture down center of tortillas. Roll up; place seam side down, on foil sheet, three to a sheet. Spoon enchilada sauce evenly over enchiladas.

3. Double fold sides and ends of foil to seal packets, leaving head space for heat circulation. Place packets on baking sheet.

4. Bake 15 minutes or until hot. Remove from oven. Carefully open packets. Sprinkle enchiladas with remaining ¼ cup cheese; bake 10 minutes more. Serve with lettuce and remaining ¼ cup tomato.

Makes 2 servings

Prep Time: 15 minutes
Cook Time: 25 minutes

Chicken, Stuffing & Green Bean Bake

  1 package (7 ounces) cubed herb-seasoned stuffing
  4 sheets (18×12 inches) heavy-duty foil, lightly sprayed with nonstick
      cooking spray
  ½ cup chicken broth
  3 cups frozen cut green beans
  4 boneless skinless chicken breasts
  1 cup chicken gravy
  ⅛ teaspoon black pepper

1. Preheat oven to 450°F.

2. Place a quarter of stuffing (1 scant cup) on one sheet of foil. Pour 2 tablespoons chicken broth over stuffing. Top stuffing with ¾ cup green beans. Place one chicken breast on top of beans. Combine gravy and pepper; pour ¼ cup over chicken.

3. Double fold sides and ends of foil to seal packets, leaving head space for heat circulation. Repeat with remaining stuffing, beans, chicken and gravy mixture to make three more packets. Place packets on baking sheet.

4. Bake 20 minutes or until chicken is no longer pink in center. Remove from oven. Carefully open one end of each packet to allow steam to escape. Open packets and transfer contents to serving plates. Serve with additional gravy, if desired. *Makes 4 servings*

Barbara's Pork Chop Dinner

Nonstick cooking spray
6 bone-in pork loin chops (¾ inch thick)
1 small onion, thinly sliced and separated into rings
6 sheets (18×12 inches) heavy-duty foil, lightly sprayed with nonstick cooking spray
6 medium red potatoes, unpeeled and cut into thin slices
1 can (10¾ ounces) condensed cream of chicken soup, undiluted
1 cup sliced fresh mushrooms
⅓ cup canned chicken broth
2 tablespoons Dijon mustard
2 cloves garlic, minced
½ teaspoon salt
½ teaspoon dried basil leaves
¼ teaspoon black pepper
Chopped fresh parsley

1. Preheat oven to 450°F.

2. Spray large nonstick skillet with cooking spray. Brown pork chops quickly on both sides. Set aside.

3. Divide onion rings into 6 portions. Place one portion of onion rings on each sheet of foil. Top with potato slices.

4. Combine soup, mushrooms, chicken broth, mustard, garlic, salt, basil and pepper in medium bowl. Pour some of soup mixture over potatoes and onion. Top with pork chops and remaining soup mixture.

5. Double fold sides and ends of foil to seal packets, leaving head space for heat circulation. Place packets on baking sheet.

6. Bake 28 to 30 minutes or until potatoes are tender. Remove packets from oven. Carefully open one end of each packet to allow steam to escape. Open packets and transfer contents to serving plates. Sprinkle with parsley.   *Makes 6 servings*

Asian Beef & Orange Packets

2 cups instant rice
4 sheets (18×12 inches) heavy-duty foil, sprayed lightly with nonstick cooking spray
1 pound lean beef flank steak, cut into short, thin strips
½ teaspoon black pepper
1 green bell pepper, cut into thin strips
1 red bell pepper, cut in thin strips
½ cup teriyaki sauce
¼ cup orange marmalade
1 can (11 ounces) mandarin orange sections, drained
8 ice cubes
1 cup beef broth or water
1 green onion, sliced (optional)

1. Preheat oven to 450°F.

2. Place ½ cup rice in center of one sheet of foil. Divide beef strips into four equal portions. Arrange four beef strips on foil to enclose rice. Top with remainder of one portion of beef. Sprinkle with ⅛ teaspoon pepper.

3. Place a quarter of bell peppers on beef. Combine teriyaki sauce and marmalade in small bowl. Drizzle 1 tablespoon teriyaki sauce mixture over vegetables.

4. Arrange a quarter of orange sections around beef and rice. Place 2 ice cubes on top of vegetables. Fold up sides of foil and pour ¼ cup broth into packet.

5. Double fold sides and ends of foil to seal packet, leaving head space for heat circulation. Repeat with remaining rice, beef, bell peppers, sauce mixture, orange sections, ice cubes and broth to make three more packets. Place packets on baking sheet.

6. Bake 20 minutes or until beef and vegetables are tender. Remove from oven. Let stand 5 minutes. Open packets and transfer contents to serving plates. Garnish with green onion, if desired. *Makes 4 servings*

Sausage, Potato and Apple Bake

3 tablespoons brown sugar
1 tablespoon dried thyme leaves
1 tablespoon dried oregano leaves
¼ cup dry white wine or apple cider
2 tablespoons cider vinegar
2 sweet potatoes (1½ to 2 pounds), peeled and cut into ¼-inch pieces
2 apples, such as Fuji or McIntosh, peeled, cored and cut into ¼-inch pieces
1 medium white onion, sliced into thin strips
1 red bell pepper, cut into thin strips
1 yellow bell pepper, cut into thin strips
½ cup golden raisins
4 sheets (18×12 inches) heavy-duty foil, lightly sprayed with nonstick cooking spray
1½ pounds smoked sausage, such as kielbasa or Polish sausage, sliced diagonally into ¼-inch pieces

1. Preheat oven to 450°F.

2. Combine sugar, thyme and oregano in large bowl. Stir in white wine and vinegar and stir until brown sugar is dissolved.

3. Add potatoes, apples, onion, bell peppers and raisins; toss to coat. Using slotted spoon, divide potato mixture evenly among foil sheets. Fold up sides of foil around potato mixture.

4. Add sausage to bowl with remaining liquid; toss to coat. Divide sausage among four foil packets. Pour any remaining marinade over sausage mixture. Double fold sides and ends of foil to seal packets. Place packets on baking sheet.

5. Bake 20 minutes or until vegetables are tender. Remove packets from oven. Carefully open one end of each pack to allow steam to escape. Open packets and transfer contents to serving plates.   *Makes 4 servings*

Chicken Divan

 1 cup instant rice
 2 sheets (18×12 inches) heavy-duty foil, lightly sprayed with nonstick
    cooking spray
 8 chicken tenders
 1½ cups broccoli florets
 ¼ cup chicken broth
 4 ice cubes
 ⅔ cup Alfredo pasta sauce
 2 tablespoons grated Parmesan cheese

1. Preheat oven to 450°F.

2. Place ½ cup rice in center of one sheet of foil. Place 4 chicken tenders on foil to enclose rice. Arrange half of broccoli on chicken. Pour 2 tablespoons chicken broth over rice. Top with two ice cubes.

3. Pour ⅓ cup sauce over chicken and broccoli. Sprinkle with 1 tablespoon cheese.

4. Double fold sides and ends of foil to seal packet, leaving head space for heat circulation. Repeat with remaining rice, chicken, broccoli, broth, ice cubes, sauce and cheese. Place packets on baking sheet.

5. Bake 15 minutes or until chicken is no longer pink in center. Remove from oven. Let stand 5 minutes. Open packets and transfer contents to serving plates.
Makes 2 servings

Summer Vegetable & Fish Bundles

4 fish fillets (about 1 pound)
1 pound thinly sliced vegetables*
1 envelope LIPTON® RECIPE SECRETS® Savory Herb with Garlic or Golden Onion Soup Mix
½ cup water

Use any combination of the following: thinly sliced mushrooms, zucchini, yellow squash or tomatoes.

On two 18×18-inch pieces heavy-duty aluminum foil, divide fish equally; top with vegetables. Evenly pour savory herb with garlic soup mix blended with water over fish. Wrap foil loosely around fillets and vegetables, sealing edges airtight with double fold. Grill or broil seam side up 15 minutes or until fish flakes when tested with fork. *Makes about 4 servings*

Menu Suggestion: Serve over hot cooked rice with Lipton® Iced Tea mixed with a splash of cranberry juice cocktail.

Melted SPAM® & Cheese Poppy Seed Sandwiches

½ cup butter or margarine, softened
3 tablespoons prepared mustard
1 tablespoon poppy seeds
8 slices cracked wheat bread
1 (12-ounce) can SPAM® Luncheon Meat, cut into 8 slices
4 (1-ounce) slices American cheese

Heat oven to 375°F. In small bowl, combine butter, mustard and poppy seeds. Spread butter mixture on bread slices. Place 2 slices of SPAM® on each of 4 bread slices. Top SPAM® with 1 slice of cheese. Top with remaining 4 bread slices. Wrap sandwiches in foil. Bake 10 to 15 minutes or until cheese is melted. *Makes 4 servings*

Stuffed Bell Peppers

  1 cup chopped fresh tomatoes
  1 teaspoon chopped fresh cilantro
½ clove garlic, finely minced
½ teaspoon dried oregano leaves, divided
¼ teaspoon ground cumin
  6 ounces lean ground round
½ cup cooked brown rice
¼ cup cholesterol-free egg substitute *or* 1 egg white
  2 tablespoons finely chopped onion
¼ teaspoon salt
⅛ teaspoon black pepper
  2 large bell peppers, any color, seeded and cut in half lengthwise
  4 sheets (12×12 inches) heavy-duty foil, lightly sprayed with nonstick
      cooking spray

1. Preheat oven to 400°F.

2. Combine tomatoes, cilantro, garlic, ¼ teaspoon oregano and cumin in small bowl. Set aside.

3. Thoroughly combine beef, rice, egg substitute, onion, salt and black pepper in large bowl. Stir ⅔ cup of tomato mixture into beef mixture. Spoon filling evenly into pepper halves.

4. Place each pepper half on foil sheet. Double fold sides and edges to seal packets. Place packets on baking sheet.

5. Bake 30 minutes or until meat is longer pink and peppers are tender. Serve with remaining tomato salsa, if desired.   *Makes 4 servings*

Steak & Gnocchi Bake

2 packages (1 pound each) gnocchi (frozen or dried)
½ pound button mushrooms
2 pounds boneless beef sirloin (1 inch thick)
   Salt
   Black pepper
¼ to ⅓ cup grated Parmesan cheese
3 tablespoons butter, softened to room temperature
3 tablespoons whole-grain mustard
½ cup steak sauce
6 to 8 sheets (18×12 inches) heavy-duty foil, lightly sprayed with nonstick
      cooking spray

1. Preheat oven to 450°F. Cook gnocchi according to package directions; drain.

2. Gently combine prepared gnocchi and mushrooms in medium bowl.

3. Cut steak across the grain into ⅛-inch slices. Season to taste with salt and pepper.

4. Combine cheese, butter, mustard and steak sauce in small bowl.

5. Place one-sixth of gnocchi mixture in center of each sheet of foil. Divide beef into six portions and arrange on top of gnocchi mixture. Divide cheese mixture into six portions and place on beef.

6. Double fold sides and ends of foil to seal packets, leaving head space for heat to circulation. Place packets on baking sheet.

7. Bake 12 to 15 minutes until beef is tender. Remove packets from oven. Carefully open one end of each packet to allow steam to escape. Open packets and transfer contents to serving plates.

Makes 6 to 8 servings

Honey-Mustard Chicken with Sauerkraut & Spuds

2 tablespoons stoneground mustard
1 tablespoon honey
2 boneless skinless chicken breasts
2 medium red potatoes, thinly sliced
2 sheets (18×12 inches) heavy-duty foil, lightly sprayed with nonstick
    cooking spray
¼ teaspoon salt
⅛ teaspoon black pepper
1½ cups fresh sauerkraut, divided
2 slices Swiss cheese
2 teaspoons minced fresh parsley *or* 1 teaspoon dried parsley flakes
Additional mustard

1. Preheat toaster oven or oven to 450°F.

2. Combine mustard and honey in medium bowl. Add chicken and turn several times to coat with mustard mixture. Let stand 10 minutes.

3. Meanwhile, divide potato slices between foil sheets, overlapping slices to form a rectangle about size of chicken breast. Sprinkle potato slices with salt and pepper.

4. Place chicken on potato slices. Top with sauerkraut and cheese slices. Sprinkle with parsley.

5. Double fold sides and ends of foil to seal packets, leaving head space for heat circulation. Place packets on toaster oven tray or baking sheet. Bake 35 to 40 minutes or until meat is cooked and potatoes are tender.

6. Remove packets from oven. Carefully open one end of packets to allow steam to escape. Open packets and transfer contents to serving plates. Serve with additional mustard. *Makes 2 servings*

Chicken with Cornbread Dumplings

4 boneless skinless chicken breasts (about 1 to 1½ pounds)
½ cup chicken broth
½ cup half-and-half
1 teaspoon salt
1 teaspoon dried thyme leaves
1 teaspoon black pepper
½ teaspoon dried sage leaves
1 red bell pepper, diced
1 can (8 ounces) cut green beans *or* 1 package (9 ounces) cut green beans, thawed and drained
1 can (8 ounces) corn, drained
4 sheets (12×12 inches) heavy-duty foil, lightly sprayed with nonstick cooking spray
1 can (11½ ounces) refrigerated cornbread twists

1. Preheat oven to 450°F. Cut chicken breasts into ¾-inch cubes.

2. Mix chicken broth, half-and-half, salt, thyme, pepper and sage in large bowl. Add chicken, bell pepper, green beans and corn; stir to coat. Divide mixture evenly among four sheets of foil, reserving liquid. Fold up sides of foil around chicken mixture.

3. Cut cornbread twists into pieces about 1 inch long; divide evenly among packets, placing cornbread pieces around outside edge of chicken mixture.

4. Adjust foil around chicken mixture, if necessary, leaving tops of packets open. Pour reserved liquid into foil packets, about 3 tablespoons per packet. Double fold sides and ends of foil to seal packets leaving head space for heat circulation. Place packets on baking sheet.

5. Bake 18 to 24 minutes or until chicken is no longer pink. Remove from oven. Carefully open one end of packets to allow steam to escape. Open packets and transfer contents to serving plates.   *Makes 4 servings*

Note: One (7-ounce) cornbread mix, prepared according to package directions, may be substituted for the refrigerated cornbread twists. Drop by rounded teaspoonfuls around edges of chicken mixture.

Tilapia & Sweet Corn Baked in Foil

⅔ cup fresh or frozen corn kernels
¼ cup finely chopped onion
¼ cup finely chopped red bell pepper
2 cloves garlic, minced
1 teaspoon chopped fresh rosemary *or* ½ teaspoon crushed dried rosemary, divided
½ teaspoon salt, divided
¼ to ½ teaspoon black pepper, divided
2 tilapia fillets (4 ounces each)
1 teaspoon olive oil
2 sheets (18×12 inches) heavy-duty foil, lightly sprayed with nonstick cooking spray

1. Preheat toaster oven or oven to 400°F.

2. Combine corn, onion, bell pepper, garlic, ½ teaspoon fresh rosemary, ¼ teaspoon salt and half the black pepper in small bowl. Spoon half the corn mixture onto each sheet of foil, spreading out slightly.

3. Arrange tilapia fillets on top of corn mixture. Brush fish with oil; sprinkle with remaining ½ teaspoon fresh rosemary, ¼ teaspoon salt and black pepper.

4. Double fold sides and ends of foil to seal packets, leaving head space for heat circulation. Place packets on toaster oven tray or on baking sheet.

5. Bake 15 minutes or until fish is opaque throughout. Remove packets from oven. Carefully open one end of each packet to allow steam to escape. Open packets and transfer contents to serving plates.

Makes 2 servings

Tip: For a special flavor, roast corn and red bell pepper on foil-lined baking sheet, lightly sprayed with nonstick cooking spray, in 450°F oven for 15 minutes or until slightly brown, stirring once. Then proceed with recipe as directed above.

Apricot Pork Chops and Dressing

1 box (6 ounces) herb-seasoned stuffing mix
½ cup dried apricots (about 16), quartered
6 sheets (18×12-inches) heavy-duty foil, lightly sprayed with nonstick cooking spray
6 bone-in pork chops, ½ inch thick
Salt
Black pepper
6 tablespoons apricot jam
1 bag (16 ounces) frozen green peas
3 cups matchstick carrots*

*Precut matchstick carrots are available in the produce section of large supermarkets.

1. Preheat oven to 450°F. Prepare stuffing mix according to package directions; stir in apricots.

2. Place ½ cup stuffing mixture in center of one sheet of foil. Place 1 pork chop over stuffing mixture, pressing down slightly and shaping stuffing to conform to shape of chop. Sprinkle chop with salt and pepper. Spread 1 tablespoon apricot jam over pork chop.

3. Place ⅔ cup peas beside pork chop in curve of bone. Arrange ½ cup carrots around outside of chop.

4. Double fold sides and ends of foil to seal packet, leaving head space for heat circulation. Repeat with remaining stuffing mixture, pork chops, salt, pepper, jam and vegetables to make 5 more packets. Place packets on baking sheet.

5. Bake 25 to 26 minutes or until pork chops and vegetables are tender. Remove from oven. Carefully open one end of each packet to allow steam to escape. Open packets and transfer contents to serving plates.

Makes 6 servings

Foil Baked Albacore

½ cup frozen peas
½ cup sliced carrot
½ cup sliced red or green bell pepper or zucchini
⅓ cup sliced onion
2 large mushrooms, sliced
1 (3-ounce) pouch of STARKIST® Solid White Tuna, drained
¼ cup bottled Italian dressing
   Salt and pepper to taste
1 large tomato, quartered
⅓ cup shredded Cheddar cheese (optional)

Combine vegetables; divide between 2 pieces (each 12 inches square) of heavy-duty foil. Divide tuna in half; mound over vegetables. Drizzle each serving with dressing; add salt and pepper. Add 2 tomato quarters to each serving; sprinkle with cheese, if desired. Fold foil into closed packet, sealing edges securely. Bake in 450°F oven 15 minutes or cook on barbecue until thoroughly heated.   *Makes 2 servings*

Prep Time: 25 minutes

SPAM™ Hot Vegetable Salad Sandwiches

6 unsliced whole wheat buns or Kaiser rolls
1 (7-ounce) can SPAM® Luncheon Meat, cubed
1 cup (4 ounces) shredded Monterey Jack cheese
1 tomato, chopped
½ cup finely chopped broccoli
½ cup thinly sliced carrots
¼ cup chopped onion
2 tablespoons peppercorn ranch-style salad dressing

Heat oven to 350°F. Cut thin slice from top of each bun; reserve. Remove soft center from each bun, leaving ½-inch shell. Combine remaining ingredients. Spoon into buns, pressing filling into buns. Top with reserved bun tops. Wrap each sandwich tightly in aluminum foil. Bake 20 minutes or until thoroughly heated and cheese is melted.   *Makes 6 servings*

Mediterranean Chicken

       4 boneless skinless chicken breasts
       4 sheets (18×12 inches) heavy-duty foil, lightly sprayed with nonstick cooking spray
    ½ teaspoon dried oregano leaves
       8 sun-dried tomatoes, cut into thin slivers
       2 jars (6 ounces each) quartered marinated artichoke hearts, drained
       1 can (about 4 ounces) sliced ripe olives, drained
 2⅔ cups cubed unpeeled baking potatoes
    ¼ cup Parmesan and garlic salad dressing
       Chopped parsley (optional)

1. Preheat oven to 450°F.

2. Place one chicken breast in center of one sheet of foil. Sprinkle with ⅛ teaspoon oregano. Top with quarter of tomatoes, artichokes and olives. Arrange ⅔ cup potatoes around the edge of chicken. Drizzle with 1 tablespoon salad dressing.

3. Double fold sides and ends of foil to seal packet, leaving head space for heat circulation. Repeat with remaining chicken, oregano, vegetables and dressing to make three more packets. Place packets on baking sheet.

4. Bake 25 minutes or until chicken is no longer pink in center. Remove packets from oven. Carefully open one end of each packet to allow steam to escape. Open packets and transfer contents to serving plates. Garnish, if desired, with chopped parsley.   *Makes 4 servings*

Spectacular Sides

Broccoli in Cheese Sauce

   1 bag (16 ounces) frozen broccoli florets
   1 sheet (24×12 inches) heavy-duty foil, lightly sprayed with nonstick cooking
      spray
   1 can (10¾ ounces) condensed Cheddar cheese soup
   1 medium red or yellow bell pepper, cut into 1-inch pieces
  ¼ cup chopped onion
  ¼ cup milk
 1½ teaspoons Worcestershire sauce
  ⅛ teaspoon black pepper

1. Preheat oven to 450°F. Place frozen broccoli in center of sheet of foil. Fold foil up around broccoli to create pan.

2. Combine soup, bell pepper, onion, milk, Worcestershire sauce and black pepper in medium bowl; stir to blend. Pour over broccoli.

3. Double fold sides and ends of foil to seal packet, leaving head space for heat circulation. Place packet on baking sheet.

4. Bake 25 minutes or until vegetables are tender. Remove from oven. Carefully open one end of packet to allow steam to escape. Open packet and transfer broccoli mixture to serving bowl. *Makes 6 servings*

Oven Roasted Potatoes and Onions with Herbs

3 pounds unpeeled red potatoes, cut into 1½-inch cubes
1 large sweet onion, such as Vidalia or Walla Walla, coarsely chopped
3 tablespoons olive oil
2 tablespoons butter, melted, or bacon drippings
3 cloves garlic, minced
¾ teaspoon salt
¾ teaspoon black pepper
⅓ cup packed chopped mixed fresh herbs, such as basil, chives, parsley, oregano, rosemary, sage, tarragon and thyme

1. Preheat oven to 450°F. Arrange potatoes and onion in large shallow foil-lined roasting pan.

2. Combine oil, butter, garlic, salt and pepper in small bowl. Drizzle over potatoes and onion; toss well to combine.

3. Bake 30 minutes. Stir and bake 10 minutes more. Add herbs; toss well. Continue baking 10 to 15 minutes or until vegetables are tender and browned. Transfer to serving bowl. Garnish with fresh rosemary, if desired.
Makes 6 servings

Dijon Garlic Bread

½ cup margarine, softened
¼ cup GREY POUPON® Dijon Mustard
1 teaspoon dried oregano leaves
1 clove garlic, crushed
1 (16-inch-long) loaf Italian bread

Preheat oven to 400°F. Blend margarine, mustard, oregano and garlic in small bowl. Slice bread crosswise into 16 slices, cutting ¾ of the way through. Spread margarine mixture on each cut side of bread. Wrap in foil. Bake 15 to 20 minutes or until heated through. *Makes 16 servings*

Zucchini Tomato Bake

1 pound eggplant, coarsely chopped
2 cups zucchini slices
2 cups mushrooms slices
3 sheets (18×12 inches) heavy-duty foil, lightly sprayed with nonstick cooking spray
2 teaspoons olive oil
½ cup chopped onion
½ cup chopped fresh fennel (optional)
2 cloves garlic, minced
1 can (14½ ounces) whole tomatoes, undrained
1 tablespoon tomato paste
2 teaspoons dried basil leaves
1 teaspoon sugar

1. Preheat oven to 400°F. Divide eggplant, zucchini and mushrooms into 3 portions. Arrange each portion on foil sheet.

2. Heat oil in small skillet over medium heat. Add onion, fennel, if desired, and garlic. Cook and stir 3 to 4 minutes or until onion is tender. Add tomatoes, tomato paste, basil and sugar. Cook and stir about 4 minutes or until sauce thickens.

3. Pour sauce over eggplant mixture. Double fold sides and ends of foil to seal packets leaving head space for heat circulation. Place packets on baking sheets. Bake 30 minutes. Remove from oven. Carefully open one end of each packet. Open and transfer contents to serving dish. Garnish as desired.

Makes 6 servings

Sweet Potato and Apple Casserole

½ **cup packed dark brown sugar**
½ **teaspoon ground cinnamon**
¼ **teaspoon ground mace or nutmeg**
 2 **pounds fresh sweet potatoes, peeled and quartered**
 1 **sheet (24×18 inches) heavy-duty foil, generously sprayed with nonstick cooking spray**
  Salt
 3 **tablespoons butter, divided**
 2 **Granny Smith apples, peeled, quartered and cored**
½ **cup granola cereal**

1. Preheat oven to 375°F. Place foil loosely in 8×8 or 9×9-inch square baking pan.

2. Mix brown sugar, cinnamon and mace in small bowl. Place ⅓ of potato slices in center of foil sheet. Sprinkle with salt to taste. Crumble half the sugar mixture over potatoes and dot with 1 tablespoon butter.

3. Slice each apple quarter into four wedges. Layer half the apples on top of potatoes. Repeat layers using potatoes, sugar mixture, butter and apples. Top with remaining potatoes and 1 tablespoon butter.

4. Double fold sides and ends of foil to seal packet, leaving head space for heat circulation. Place packet on baking sheet.

5. Bake 25 minutes. Remove packets from oven. Carefully open one end of packet to allow steam to escape. Open top of packet; spoon liquid in bottom of packet over potatoes. Sprinkle with granola; do not reseal packet. Bake 35 minutes more or until potatoes are fork-tender. Garnish, if desired.   *Makes 6 servings*

Glazed Maple Acorn Squash

1 large acorn or golden acorn squash
¼ cup water
2 tablespoons pure maple syrup
1 tablespoon margarine or butter, melted
¼ teaspoon ground cinnamon
1 sheet (24×18 inches) heavy-duty foil, lightly sprayed with nonstick cooking spray

1. Preheat oven to 375°F.

2. Cut ends from squash. Cut squash crosswise into four equal slices. Discard seeds and membrane. Place squash on foil sheet. Fold sides of foil up around squash. Add water.

3. Double fold sides and ends of foil to seal packet, leaving head space for heat circulation. Place packet on baking sheet. Bake 30 minutes or until tender. Remove packet from oven.

4. Combine syrup, margarine and cinnamon in small bowl; mix well. Carefully open one end of packet to allow steam to escape and pour off water. Open top of packet. Brush squash with syrup mixture, letting excess pool in center of squash. Do not reseal packet.

5. Return packet to oven; bake 10 minutes or until syrup mixture is bubbly. Transfer contents of packet to serving dish. *Makes 4 servings*

Green Beans with Savory Mushroom Sauce

2 packages (10 ounces each) frozen French-style green beans, thawed
1 can (10¾ ounces) condensed cream of mushroom soup, undiluted
2 tablespoons dry vermouth or dry white wine
1½ cups mushrooms, sliced
½ teaspoon salt
½ teaspoon dried thyme leaves
¼ teaspoon black pepper
2 sheets (18×12 inches) heavy-duty foil, lightly sprayed with nonstick cooking spray
1 cup crushed prepared croutons or canned fried onion rings

1. Preheat oven to 450°F. Mix all ingredients except foil and croutons in large bowl. Divide mixture between foil sheets. Double fold sides and ends of foil to seal packets. Place packets on baking sheet.

2. Bake 20 minutes or until hot. Remove from oven. Carefully open one end of each packet. Open packets and transfer contents to serving dish. Sprinkle with croutons. *Makes 6 to 8 servings*

Chutney'd Squash Circles

2 acorn squash (1 pound each)
1 sheet (18×18 inches) heavy-duty foil
2 tablespoons butter or margarine
½ cup prepared chutney

1. Preheat oven to 400°F. Slice tip and stem end from squash. Scoop out and discard seeds. Cut squash crosswise into ¾-inch rings.

2. Center foil in 13×9-inch baking pan. Dot foil with butter and place squash on butter, slightly overlapping rings. Spoon chutney over slices and sprinkle with 2 tablespoons water. Double fold sides and ends of foil to seal packet, leaving head space for heat circulation.

3. Bake foil packet in baking pan 20 to 30 minutes until squash is fork-tender. Carefully open one end of packet to allow steam to escape. Open packet and transfer to warm serving plate. Pour pan drippings over squash. Garnish, if desired. *Makes 4 servings*

Potatoes au Gratin

2 medium unpeeled baking potatoes (about 1 pound)
2 sheets (18 × 18 inches) heavy-duty foil, lightly sprayed with nonstick cooking spray
1 cup (4 ounces) shredded Cheddar cheese
½ cup (2 ounces) shredded Swiss cheese
1 tablespoon butter or margarine
1 tablespoon plus 1½ teaspoons all-purpose flour
1 cup milk
1 tablespoon Dijon mustard
⅛ teaspoon salt
⅛ teaspoon black pepper

1. Preheat oven to 400°F.

2. Cut potatoes into thin slices. Arrange a quarter of potatoes on each sheet of foil. Top with half the cheeses. Repeat layers. Fold foil up around potatoes.

3. Melt butter in medium saucepan over medium heat. Stir in flour; cook 1 minute. Stir in milk, mustard, salt and pepper; bring to a boil. Reduce heat and cook, stirring constantly, until mixture thickens. Pour milk mixture over cheese.

4. Double fold sides and ends of foil to seal packets. Place packets on baking sheet.

5. Bake 25 minutes. Remove packets from oven. Carefully open tops of packets. Return to oven and bake 10 minutes more until potatoes are tender and tops are brown. Remove from oven and let stand 5 minutes before serving.

Makes 2 servings

Garden Fresh Vegetable Bundles

6 large sheets of heavy aluminum foil
  WESSON® No-Stick Cooking Spray
2 cups cubed potatoes (1-inch squares)
2 cups sliced zucchini (2-inch slices)
1 cup sliced carrots (¼-inch slices)
1 cup diced red bell pepper (1-inch dice)
1 cup diced green bell pepper (1-inch dice)
1 cup broccoli florets (1-inch pieces)
1 cup diced sweet onion (1-inch dice)
1 large ear of corn, cut into 6 pieces
¼ cup WESSON® Vegetable Oil
3 teaspoons Creole seasoning
  Garlic salt

Preheat oven to 450°F. Spray *each* sheet of foil with Wesson® Cooking Spray. In a large bowl, combine *next* 8 ingredients, ending with corn. Toss with Wesson® Oil. Evenly divide vegetable mixture among prepared sheets of foil. Sprinkle ½ teaspoon Creole seasoning on *each* vegetable packet. Sprinkle with desired amount of garlic salt. Bring sides of foil to center and fold over to seal. Fold ends to center, creating a tight bundle. Repeat with *remaining* packets. Place bundles on cookie sheet; bake for 30 minutes or until vegetables are tender. *Makes 6 servings*

Tip: This recipe also works great on the grill!

EASY FOIL Recipes

Fire Up the Grill

Grilled Potato Salad

    1 envelope LIPTON® RECIPE SECRETS® Onion Soup Mix*
    ⅓ cup olive or vegetable oil
    2 tablespoons red wine vinegar
    1 clove garlic, finely chopped
    2 pounds small red or all-purpose potatoes, cut into 1-inch cubes
    1 tablespoon chopped fresh basil *or* 1 teaspoon dried basil leaves
      Freshly ground black pepper

*Also terrific with LIPTON® RECIPE SECRETS® Onion-Mushroom or Golden Onion Soup Mix.

1. In large bowl, blend soup mix, oil, vinegar and garlic; stir in potatoes.

2. Grease 30×18-inch sheet of heavy-duty aluminum foil; top with potato mixture. Wrap foil loosely around mixture, sealing edges airtight with double fold. Place on another sheet of 30×18-inch foil; seal edges airtight with double fold in opposite direction.

3. Grill, shaking package occasionally and turning package once, 40 minutes or until potatoes are tender. Spoon into serving bowl and toss with basil and pepper. Serve slightly warm or at room temperature.

Makes 4 servings

Oven Method: Preheat oven to 450°F. Prepare foil packet as above. Place in large baking pan on bottom rack and bake, turning packet once, 40 minutes or until potatoes are tender. Toss and serve as above.

Sweet & Sour Chicken

2 boneless skinless chicken breasts
2 sheets (18×12 inches) heavy-duty foil, lightly sprayed with nonstick
  cooking spray
Salt and black pepper
½ medium green bell pepper, cut in short, thin strips
½ medium red bell pepper, cut in short, thin strips
¼ onion, cut in thin wedges
½ cup drained canned pineapple chunks
½ cup orange marmalade
1 tablespoon white vinegar
2 teaspoons cornstarch
2 teaspoons soy sauce
Hot cooked rice (optional)

1. Prepare grill for direct cooking or preheat oven to 450°F.

2. Place one chicken breast in center of one sheet of foil. Season to taste with salt and pepper.

3. Place half of bell peppers and onion on chicken breast. Top with half of pineapple chunks.

4. Combine marmalade, vinegar, cornstarch and soy sauce in small bowl; stir until cornstarch is dissolved. Pour half over vegetables.

5. Double fold sides and ends of foil to seal packets, leaving head space for heat circulation. Repeat with remaining chicken, vegetables, pineapple and sauce mixture. Place packets on baking sheet.

6. Slide packets off baking sheet onto grid of covered grill. Grill 12 to 14 minutes over medium-high coals until chicken is no longer pink in center. Or, bake packets on baking sheet 16 to 18 minutes. Carefully open one end of each packet to allow steam to escape. Open packets and transfer mixture to serving plates. Serve with rice, if desired.

Makes 2 servings

Grilled Paella

1½ to 2 pounds chicken wings or thighs
2 tablespoons plus ¼ cup extra-virgin olive oil, divided
  Salt and black pepper
1 pound garlicky sausage links, such as linguisa, chorizo or Italian
1 large onion, chopped
2 large red bell peppers, seeded and cut into thin strips
4 cloves garlic, minced
1 can (14 ounces) diced tomatoes, undrained
4 cups uncooked rice
16 tightly closed live mussels or clams,* scrubbed
½ pound large shrimp,* peeled and deveined with tails intact
1½ cups frozen peas
1 can (about 14 ounces) chicken broth
2 lemons, cut into wedges
1 oval disposable foil pan (about 17×13×3 inches)

*Seafood can be omitted; add an additional 1¼ to 1½ pounds chicken.

Brush chicken with 2 tablespoons oil; season with salt and black pepper. Grill chicken and sausage on covered grill over medium KINGSFORD® Briquets 15 to 20 minutes or until chicken juices run clear and sausage is no longer pink, turning every 5 minutes. Cut sausage into 2-inch pieces.

Heat remaining ¼ cup oil in large skillet over medium-high heat. Add onion, bell peppers and garlic; cook and stir 5 minutes or until vegetables are tender. Add tomatoes, 1½ teaspoons salt and ½ teaspoon black pepper; cook about 8 minutes until thick, stirring frequently. Combine onion mixture and rice in foil pan; spread evenly. Arrange chicken, sausage, seafood and peas over rice. Bring broth and 6 cups water to a boil in 3 quart saucepan. Place foil pan on grid over medium KINGSFORD® briquets; immediately pour boiling broth mixture over rice. Grill on covered grill about 20 minutes until liquid is absorbed. *Do not stir.* Cover with foil; let stand 10 minutes. Garnish with lemon wedges.

Makes 8 to 10 servings

"Grilled" Tuna with Vegetables in Herb Butter

4 pieces heavy-duty aluminum foil, each 18×12 inches
1 can (12 ounces) STARKIST® Tuna, drained and broken into chunks
1 cup slivered red or green bell pepper
1 cup slivered yellow squash or zucchini
1 cup pea pods, cut crosswise into halves
1 cup slivered carrots
4 green onions, cut into 2-inch slices
   Salt and black pepper to taste (optional)

Herb Butter
3 tablespoons butter or margarine, melted
1 tablespoon lemon or lime juice
1 clove garlic, minced
2 teaspoons dried tarragon leaves, crushed
1 teaspoon dried dill weed

On each piece of foil, mound tuna, bell pepper, squash, pea pods, carrots and onions. Sprinkle with salt and black pepper.

For Herb Butter, in small bowl stir together butter, lemon juice, garlic, tarragon and dill. Drizzle over tuna and vegetables. Fold edges of each foil square together to make packets.

To grill
Place foil packets about 4 inches above hot coals. Grill for 10 to 12 minutes or until heated through, turning packets over halfway through grill time.

To bake
Place foil packets on baking sheet. Bake in preheated 450°F oven for 15 to 20 minutes or until heated through.

To serve
Cut an "X" on top of each packet; peel back foil.   *Makes 4 servings*

Easy Pepper Steak & Rice

1 cup instant rice

4 sheets (18×12 inches) heavy-duty foil, lightly sprayed with nonstick
   cooking spray

1 pound beef sirloin steak (1 inch thick), cut into thin strips

¼ cup teriyaki sauce

1 tablespoon plus 1 teaspoon ketchup

1 clove garlic, minced

½ cup canned beef broth

8 ice cubes

1 cup chopped onion

1 large green or red bell pepper, cut in short strips

1. Prepare grill for direct cooking or preheat oven to 450°F.

2. Place ¼ cup rice in center of one sheet of foil. Place beef strips in medium bowl. Combine teriyaki sauce, ketchup and garlic in small bowl; mix well. Pour over beef and mix until beef is coated with sauce.

3. Divide beef into four portions. Arrange four beef strips on foil to enclose rice. Pour 2 tablespoons broth over rice. Top with two ice cubes.

4. Arrange remainder of one portion of beef on ice cubes and rice. Top with a quarter of onion and bell pepper.

5. Double fold sides and ends of foil to seal packet, leaving head space for heat circulation. Repeat with remaining rice, beef, broth, ice cubes and vegetables to make three more packets. Place packets on baking sheet.

6. Slide packets off baking sheet onto grid of covered grill. Grill 12 to 13 minutes over medium-high coals. Or, bake on baking sheet 14 to 15 minutes. Remove from oven. Let stand 5 minutes. Open packets and transfer contents to serving plates.   *Makes 4 servings*

Grilled Sweet Potato Packets with Pecan Butter

4 sweet potatoes (about 8 ounces each), peeled and cut into ¼-inch slices
1 large sweet or Spanish onion, thinly sliced and separated into rings
3 tablespoons vegetable oil
⅓ cup butter or margarine, softened
2 tablespoons packed light brown sugar
¼ teaspoon salt
¼ teaspoon ground cinnamon
¼ cup chopped pecans, toasted

1. Prepare barbecue grill for direct cooking.

2. Alternately place potato slices and onion rings on four 14×12-inch sheets of heavy-duty foil. Brush tops and sides with oil to prevent drying.

3. Double fold sides and ends of foil to seal packets. Place foil packets on grid. Grill packets, on covered grill, over medium coals 25 to 30 minutes or until potatoes are fork-tender.

4. Meanwhile, to prepare Pecan Butter, combine butter, sugar, salt and cinnamon in small bowl; mix well. Stir in pecans. Open packets carefully; top each with dollop of Pecan Butter. *Makes 4 servings*

Grilled Banana Squash with Rum & Brown Sugar

2 pounds banana squash or butternut squash
2 tablespoons dark rum or apple juice
2 tablespoons melted butter
2 tablespoons brown sugar

Cut squash into 4 pieces; discard seeds. Place squash in microwavable baking dish. Cover with vented plastic wrap. Microwave at HIGH 5 to 7 minutes, turning once. Discard plastic wrap; pierce flesh of squash with fork at 1-inch intervals. Place squash in foil pan. Combine rum and butter; brush over squash. Sprinkle with sugar. Grill squash on covered grill over medium KINGSFORD® Briquets 20 to 30 minutes until squash is tender. *Makes 4 servings*

Herbed Mushroom Vegetable Medley

4 ounces button or cremini mushrooms, sliced
1 medium red or yellow bell pepper, cut into ¼-inch-wide strips
1 medium zucchini, cut crosswise into ¼-inch-thick slices
1 medium yellow squash, cut crosswise into ¼-inch-thick slices
3 tablespoons butter or margarine, melted
1 tablespoon chopped fresh thyme leaves *or* 1 teaspoon dried thyme leaves
1 tablespoon chopped fresh basil leaves *or* 1 teaspoon dried basil leaves
1 tablespoon chopped fresh chives or green onion tops
1 clove garlic, minced
¼ teaspoon salt
¼ teaspoon black pepper

1. Prepare barbecue grill for direct cooking.

2. Combine mushrooms, bell pepper, zucchini and squash in large bowl. Combine butter, thyme, basil, chives, garlic, salt and black pepper in small bowl. Pour over vegetable mixture; toss to coat well.

3. Transfer mixture to 20×14-inch sheet of heavy-duty foil. Double fold sides and ends to seal packet, leaving head space for heat circulation. Place foil packet on grid. Grill packet, on covered grill, over medium coals 20 to 25 minutes or until vegetables are fork-tender. Carefully open one end of packet to allow steam to escape. Open packet and transfer contents to serving dish. *Makes 4 to 6 servings*

Savory Grilled Potatoes in Foil

  ½ cup MIRACLE WHIP® Salad Dressing
   1 teaspoon garlic powder *or* 3 garlic cloves, minced
  ½ teaspoon paprika
  ¼ teaspoon salt
  ¼ teaspoon black pepper
   3 baking potatoes, cut into ¼-inch slices
   1 large onion, sliced

MIX salad dressing and seasonings in large bowl until well blended. Add potatoes and onion; toss to coat.

DIVIDE potato mixture evenly among 6 (12-inch) square pieces of foil. Seal each to form packet. Place foil packets on grill over medium-hot coals.

GRILL covered, 25 to 30 minutes or until potatoes are tender.

Makes 6 servings

Use Your Oven: Assemble foil packets as directed. Place on center rack in oven. Bake at 425°F for 40 to 45 minutes or until potatoes are tender.

Prep: 15 minutes
Grill: 30 minutes

Backyard S'Mores

   2 milk chocolate bars (1.55 ounces each), cut in half
   8 large marshmallows
   4 whole graham crackers (8 squares)

Place each chocolate bar half and 2 marshmallows between 2 graham cracker squares. Wrap in lightly greased foil. Place on grill over medium-low KINGSFORD® Briquets about 3 to 5 minutes or until chocolate and marshmallows are melted. (Time will vary depending upon how hot coals are and whether grill is open or covered.) *Makes 4 servings*

Trout Stuffed with Fresh Mint and Oranges

2 pan-dressed* trout (1 to 1¼ pounds each)
½ teaspoon coarse salt, such as Kosher salt
1 orange, sliced
1 cup fresh mint leaves
1 sweet onion, sliced

*A pan-dressed trout has been gutted and scaled with head and tail removed.

1. Rinse trout under cold running water; pat dry with paper towels.

2. Sprinkle cavities of trout with salt; fill each with orange slices and mint. Cover each fish with onion slices.

3. Spray 2 large sheets of foil with nonstick cooking spray. Place 1 fish on each sheet. Double fold sides and ends of foil to seal packets, leaving head space for heat circulation.

4. Place foil packets, seam side down, directly on medium-hot coals; grill on covered grill 20 to 25 minutes or until trout flakes easily when tested with fork, turning once.

5. Carefully open one end of each foil packet to allow steam to escape. Remove and discard orange-mint stuffing. Serve immediately.

Makes 6 servings

Cheddary Pull Apart Bread

1 round loaf corn or sour dough bread (1 pound)*
½ cup (1 stick) butter or margarine, melted
¼ cup *French's*® Classic Yellow® Mustard
½ teaspoon chili powder
½ teaspoon seasoned salt
¼ teaspoon garlic powder
1 cup (4 ounces) shredded Cheddar cheese

You may substitute one 12-inch loaf Italian bread for the corn bread.

Cut bread into 1-inch slices, cutting about ⅔ of the way down through loaf. (Do not cut through bottom crust.) Turn bread ¼ turn and cut across slices in similar fashion. Combine butter, mustard and seasonings in small bowl until blended. Brush cut surfaces of bread with butter mixture. Spread bread "sticks" apart and sprinkle cheese inside. Wrap loaf in foil.

Place packet on grid. Cook over medium coals about 30 minutes or until bread is toasted and cheese melts. Pull bread "sticks" apart to serve.

Makes about 8 servings

Prep Time: 15 minutes
Cook Time: 30 minutes

Quick Tip

This recipe may be prepared up to 12 hours ahead of time, wrapped in foil and refrigerated until 30 minutes before you plan to serve dinner. Simply add an additional five minutes to the grilling time.

Vegetable-Topped Fish Pouches

4 firm fish fillets, such as flounder, cod or halibut (about 1 pound)
1 carrot, cut into very thin strips
1 rib celery, cut into very thin strips
1 medium red onion, cut into thin wedges
1 medium zucchini or yellow squash, sliced
8 mushrooms, sliced
½ cup (about 2 ounces) shredded Swiss cheese
½ cup WISH-BONE® Italian Dressing*

Also terrific with Wish-Bone® Robusto Italian or Just 2 Good Italian Dressing.

On four 18×9-inch pieces heavy-duty aluminum foil, divide fish equally. Evenly top with vegetables, then cheese. Drizzle with Italian dressing. Wrap foil loosely around fillets and vegetables, sealing edges airtight with double fold. Let stand to marinate 15 minutes. Grill or broil pouches, seam sides up, 15 minutes or until fish flakes easily with fork.

Makes 4 servings

Lemon 'n' Dill Barbecued Corn-on-the-Cob

6 medium (8 to 12 ounces each) unhusked whole ears corn
3 tablespoons soft (50% reduced-calorie) margarine
Grated peel of ½ SUNKIST® lemon
1 tablespoon fresh squeezed juice from 1 SUNKIST® lemon
1 tablespoon chopped fresh dill *or* 1 teaspoon dry dill weed
Salt and white pepper to taste

Carefully pull back husks (do not detach) and remove silk from each ear of corn. Rinse well in cold water. In small bowl, beat margarine, lemon peel and lemon juice until well blended. Stir in dill. To prepare each ear of corn, place on 12- to 16-inch-long piece of foil; brush corn with ⅙ of margarine mixture. Sprinkle lightly with salt and pepper. Replace husks around corn; individually wrap each securely in foil. Grill 6 inches above glowing coals or on MEDIUM heat of gas barbecue 25 to 35 minutes, turning every 5 minutes. To serve, remove foil and cut off husks.   *Makes 6 servings*

Baked Cinnamon Apples

4 medium Granny Smith or Rome Beauty apples
4 sheets (18×12 inches) heavy-duty foil, lightly sprayed with nonstick cooking spray
⅓ cup brown sugar, packed
¼ cup dried cranberries
½ teaspoon ground cinnamon
2 tablespoons butter, cut into 4 pieces
Vanilla ice cream

1. Preheat oven to 450°F. Core apples. Using paring knife, trim off ½-inch strip around top of each apple. Place each apple in center of foil sheet.

2. Mix brown sugar, cranberries and cinnamon in small bowl. Fill apples with sugar mixture, sprinkling any excess around pared rim. Place 1 piece butter on sugar mixture; press gently.

3. Double fold sides and ends of foil to seal packets, leaving head space for heat circulation. Place packets on baking sheet.

4. Bake 20 minutes. Remove from oven. Carefully open foil packets; shape foil around apples. Bake 10 minutes more or until apples are tender. Remove from oven. Transfer apples to bowls; spoon remaining liquid over apples. Serve warm apples with ice cream.   *Makes 4 servings*

Chocolate Frosted Peanut Butter Cupcakes

⅓ cup creamy or chunky peanut butter
⅓ cup butter, softened
½ cup granulated sugar
¼ cup firmly packed brown sugar
2 eggs
1 teaspoon vanilla
1¾ cups all-purpose flour
1½ teaspoons baking powder
½ teaspoon salt
1¼ cups milk
Peanut Butter Chocolate Frosting (recipe follows)

1. Preheat oven to 350°F. Line 18 (2½-inch) muffin cups with foil or paper baking cups.

2. Beat peanut butter and butter at medium speed in large bowl of electric mixer until smooth; beat in sugars until fluffy. Beat in eggs and vanilla.

3. Combine flour, baking powder and salt in medium bowl. Add flour mixture to peanut butter mixture alternately with milk, beginning and ending with flour mixture.

4. Spoon batter into prepared muffin cups. Bake 23 to 25 minutes or until cupcakes spring back when touched and wooden pick inserted into centers comes out clean. Cool in pans on wire racks 10 minutes; remove from pans and cool completely.

5. Prepare Peanut Butter Chocolate Frosting. Frost each cupcake with frosting. *Makes 1½ dozen cupcakes*

Peanut Butter Chocolate Frosting: Combine 4 cups powdered sugar, ⅓ cup unsweetened cocoa powder, 4 tablespoons milk and 3 tablespoons creamy peanut butter; beat until well blended, adding additional milk, 1 tablespoon at a time, until desired consistency.

Cinnamon-Raisin-Banana Bread Pudding

  1 egg, beaten
  2 tablespoons light brown sugar
  1 tablespoon half-and-half or undiluated evaporated milk
  ¼ teaspoon cinnamon
  ¼ teaspoon vanilla
  1 banana
  1 tablespoon lemon juice
  3 slices cinnamon-raisin bread
  1 sheet (18×12 inches) heavy-duty foil, generously sprayed with nonstick
    cooking spray
  2 teaspoons butter, softened and divided
  2 tablespoons reduced-fat spreadable cream cheese, divided
  1 tablespoon raisins
    Vanilla ice cream (optional)

1. Preheat oven or toaster oven to 350°F.

2. Mix together egg, brown sugar, half-and-half, cinnamon and vanilla in small bowl. Set aside.

3. Peel and chop banana; place in small bowl. Sprinkle with lemon juice and set aside.

4. Butter one side of one slice of bread with 1 teaspoon butter. Lay bread, buttered side down, on foil. Spread bread slice with 1 tablespoon cream cheese. Fold foil edges up to form close-fitting container around bread.

5. Spoon 2 tablespoons egg mixture onto bread slice. Arrange half the banana cubes on bread. Sprinkle with half the raisins. Spread remaining 1 tablespoon cream cheese on one side of one piece of bread. Place bread slice on bananas, cream cheese side down. Spoon 2 tablespoons egg mixture over bread slice. Top with remaining banana and raisins. Spread remaining 1 teaspoon butter on one side of remaining bread slice. Cut bread slice into cubes. Place bread cubes on banana. Drizzle remaining egg mixture over bread cubes. Do not seal foil container.

6. Place foil container on baking sheet. Bake 30 minutes or until pudding is set and top is golden brown and crusty. Remove from oven. Transfer bread pudding to serving plates. Serve with ice cream, if desired.

Makes 2 to 3 servings

Spiced Pear with Vanilla Ice Cream

1 sheet (18×12 inches) heavy-duty foil
2 teaspoons butter, softened
1 tablespoon light brown sugar
¼ teaspoon pumpkin pie spice
1 large Bosc pear, halved lengthwise and cored
Lemon juice
2 scoops vanilla ice cream

1. Preheat toaster oven or oven to 450°F. Coat center of foil with butter.

2. Combine sugar and pumpkin pie spice in small bowl. Sprinkle sugar mixture over butter. Sprinkle cut sides of pear halves with lemon juice. Place pear halves, cut side down, side by side on sugar mixture.

3. Double fold sides and ends of foil to seal foil packet, leaving head space for heat circulation. Place packet on toaster oven tray or baking sheet.

4. Bake 40 minutes or until pear halves are tender. Remove from oven. Let stand 15 minutes.

5. Open packet and transfer pear halves to serving plates. Spoon sauce over pears. Serve with ice cream.   *Makes 2 servings*

Quick Tip

An Anjou or Bartlett pear may be substituted for the Bosc pear, if desired. For a more compact packet, place pear halves side by side with the narrow tip of one half adjacent to the broad base of the other pear half.

Easy Gingerbread

1 sheet (24×12 inches) heavy-duty foil
1 cup all-purpose flour
⅓ cup firmly packed brown sugar
1 teaspoon ground ginger
¾ teaspoon ground cinnamon
½ teaspoon baking soda
½ teaspoon baking powder
¼ teaspoon salt
¼ teaspoon ground cloves
1 egg
½ cup milk
⅓ cup melted butter
¼ cup unsulphured molasses
Powdered sugar (optional)

1. Preheat oven to 350°F. Center foil over 8×5×2½-inch loaf pan. Gently ease foil into pan. You will have a 1-inch overhang of foil on sides and a 5-inch overhang on ends. Generously spray foil with nonstick cooking spray.

2. Combine flour, brown sugar, ginger, cinnamon, baking soda, baking powder, salt and cloves in medium bowl; mix well.

3. In separate small bowl, beat egg. Stir in milk, butter and molasses until well mixed.

4. Add liquid mixture to dry ingredients; stir until smooth. Pour batter into foil-lined pan. Fold overhanging foil sides over batter to cover batter completely; crimp foil, leaving head space for cake as it rises.

5. Bake 45 minutes or until wooden pick inserted in center comes out clean. Remove from oven. Carefully open foil to allow steam to escape. Cool in pan on wire rack 10 to 15 minutes. Place serving plate over pan and invert gingerbread onto plate. Peel off foil.

6. Serve warm, or at room temperature sprinkled with powdered sugar, if desired.

Makes 6 servings

Broiled Pineapple with Spiced Vanilla Sauce

   3 ounces reduced-fat cream cheese
   ¼ cup granulated sugar
   ¼ cup undiluted evaporated milk or half-and-half
   ¼ teaspoon pumpkin pie spice or Chinese 5-spice powder
   ¼ teaspoon vanilla
   1 sheet (14×12 inches) heavy-duty foil
   2 teaspoons butter
   2 thick, round slices fresh pineapple, skin and eyes trimmed
   1 tablespoon light brown sugar

1. Preheat broiler.

2. Place cream cheese, granulated sugar, milk, pumpkin pie spice and vanilla in food processor or blender; process until smooth. Refrigerate.

3. Coat center of foil sheet with butter. Place pineapple slices side by side on foil. Sprinkle with brown sugar. Fold up sides and ends of foil form container around pineapple, leaving top of container open. Place container on baking sheet.

4. Broil pineapple 4 inches from heat source 10 to 12 minutes until surface of pineapple is bubbling and flecked with brown. Watch pineapple closely during last 5 minutes of broiling to avoid burning.

5. Remove from oven. Transfer pineapple to serving plates. Serve immediately with cream cheese mixture.   *Makes 2 servings*

Chocolate Bread Pudding

1 sheet (12×12 inches) heavy-duty foil
4 slices firm-textured white bread
1 egg
1 tablespoon unsweetened cocoa powder
¾ cup milk
3 tablespoons sugar
1 teaspoon vanilla
⅛ teaspoon ground cinnamon
⅓ cup semisweet chocolate chips
Whipped topping or sweetened whipped cream (optional)

1. Preheat oven to 350°F. Generously spray center of foil with nonstick cooking spray. Toast bread just enough to dry it, but not enough to brown it. Cool slightly and cut into cubes.

2. Beat egg in large bowl; whisk in cocoa until well blended. Stir in milk, sugar, vanilla and cinnamon. Add bread cubes and chocolate chips; stir until all bread cubes are moistened. Let stand until most of liquid is absorbed.

3. Place a portion of bread cube mixture in center of foil. Carefully shape foil up and around bread cubes to form bowl about 4-inches in diameter. Add remainder of bread cube mixture. Adjust foil, if necessary, leaving foil bowl open at top. Place foil bowl on baking sheet.

4. Bake 35 to 40 minutes or until set. Remove from oven. Cool 15 minutes. Serve warm or at room temperature garnished with whipped topping, if desired. *Makes 4 servings*

Note: If desired, chocolate milk may be substituted for milk and cocoa. Cinnamon bread may be substituted for white bread; omit ground cinnamon.

Acknowledgments

The publisher would like to thank the companies and organizations listed below for the use of their recipes and photographs in this publication.

ConAgra Grocery Products Company

Grey Poupon® Dijon Mustard

Hormel Foods, LLC

The Kingsford Products Company

Kraft Foods Holdings

Lawry's® Foods, Inc.

National Chicken Council

Reckitt Benckiser

StarKist® Seafood Company

Sunkist Growers

Tyson Foods, Inc.

Uncle Ben's Inc.

Unilever Bestfoods North America

METRIC CONVERSION CHART

VOLUME MEASUREMENTS (dry)

$\frac{1}{8}$ teaspoon = 0.5 mL
$\frac{1}{4}$ teaspoon = 1 mL
$\frac{1}{2}$ teaspoon = 2 mL
$\frac{3}{4}$ teaspoon = 4 mL
1 teaspoon = 5 mL
1 tablespoon = 15 mL
2 tablespoons = 30 mL
$\frac{1}{4}$ cup = 60 mL
$\frac{1}{3}$ cup = 75 mL
$\frac{1}{2}$ cup = 125 mL
$\frac{2}{3}$ cup = 150 mL
$\frac{3}{4}$ cup = 175 mL
1 cup = 250 mL
2 cups = 1 pint = 500 mL
3 cups = 750 mL
4 cups = 1 quart = 1 L

VOLUME MEASUREMENTS (fluid)

1 fluid ounce (2 tablespoons) = 30 mL
4 fluid ounces ($\frac{1}{2}$ cup) = 125 mL
8 fluid ounces (1 cup) = 250 mL
12 fluid ounces (1$\frac{1}{2}$ cups) = 375 mL
16 fluid ounces (2 cups) = 500 mL

WEIGHTS (mass)

$\frac{1}{2}$ ounce = 15 g
1 ounce = 30 g
3 ounces = 90 g
4 ounces = 120 g
8 ounces = 225 g
10 ounces = 285 g
12 ounces = 360 g
16 ounces = 1 pound = 450 g

DIMENSIONS

$\frac{1}{16}$ inch = 2 mm
$\frac{1}{8}$ inch = 3 mm
$\frac{1}{4}$ inch = 6 mm
$\frac{1}{2}$ inch = 1.5 cm
$\frac{3}{4}$ inch = 2 cm
1 inch = 2.5 cm

OVEN TEMPERATURES

250°F = 120°C
275°F = 140°C
300°F = 150°C
325°F = 160°C
350°F = 180°C
375°F = 190°C
400°F = 200°C
425°F = 220°C
450°F = 230°C

BAKING PAN SIZES

Utensil	Size in Inches/Quarts	Metric Volume	Size in Centimeters
Baking or Cake Pan (square or rectangular)	8×8×2	2 L	20×20×5
	9×9×2	2.5 L	23×23×5
	12×8×2	3 L	30×20×5
	13×9×2	3.5 L	33×23×5
Loaf Pan	8×4×3	1.5 L	20×10×7
	9×5×3	2 L	23×13×7
Round Layer Cake Pan	8×1½	1.2 L	20×4
	9×1½	1.5 L	23×4
Pie Plate	8×1¼	750 mL	20×3
	9×1¼	1 L	23×3
Baking Dish or Casserole	1 quart	1 L	—
	1½ quart	1.5 L	—
	2 quart	2 L	—